My Chocolate Sarcophagus

POEMS

by

CLAUDIA
CARLSON

MARSH HAWK PRESS

2015

Cover sculptured art by Christina Carlson
Cover stock imagery © avain (123rf.com) and Yap Kee Chan (dreamstime.com)
Author photos by Flash Rosenburg

First Edition 10 9 8 7 6 5 4 3 2 1

Marsh Hawk Press books are published by Poetry Mailing List, Inc., a not-for-profit
corporation under section 501(c)3 United States Internal Revenue Code.

The text of this book is set in Goudy Oldstyle.

Book design by Heather Wood
www.heatherwoodbooks.com

The author gratefully acknowledges permissions to reprint:
"First MRI" and "Hospitality"
published in The Southampton Review, 2015
The winter edition of TSR: The Southampton Review (Vol. X No. I)

ISBN: 978-0-9964275-2-4

Marsh Hawk Press
P.O. Box 206
East Rockaway, New York 11518-0206
www.marshhawkpress.org

Dedicated to
my beloved family and friends,
and husband Jim.

THE LOVE THAT UNITED US
WAS ALL OUR JOY

—EPITAPH ON HELOISE'S TOMB
AT PÈRE LACHAISE

Contents

My
Chocolate
Sarcophagus

Wellspring

I am giving things away
Love mostly

Too big clothes
Books.

It feels so good
My heart does not empty.

First MRI

There's a swarm in the tunnel
I'm the branch they try to land on
a wind of reckoning keeps us apart

close my eyes and the bees
are hived for winter
shivering around the honey

stillness in the roar
the hum is louder than think...
I watch bees pulse in and out of clover

it could be summer again
I could be well.

Hospitality

I'm drowsy as I check into
The Porch at the End of the World

Hammocks and swing seats creak at the views
of pond, hills, a road frilled with wildflowers.

It's only when they serve tea, timers beeping,
tinctured with disinfectant, I remember why

I pace with other guests in our green gowns
and bracelets of tubes.

We discuss sunsets with authority
when we are hale enough to rise and see them.

If only true scents lifted from the waters and trees
or a breeze to dry my damp hair.

How are you?

I'm tired of *how are you?* Schadenfreude thrill
of knowing I'm the one who's terminally...
Oh fuck it! The Grim Reaper will kill
daisies, hard drives, you, eventually.
Yes my lungs are filled with little tumors
telling you makes it hard to breathe.

Chocolate Sarcophagus

I'm eating chocolates shaped like the filigree
of a whore's garter belt. Lascivious as the dark
spit I lick across your nipple, orgy with flesh
of cream locked into seared pulverized beans.

At first, bitter as disappointed meditation,
then the sweetened meat of it melts,
velvety, into the box seat of my mouth.
OM to addicted synapse, a trick, a gift, a thrill...
cocaine's love surge marveled by caffeine's quickening.

"Sugar is unhealthy, you know, makes cancer grow."
Shall I marry a brussels sprout, write hymns to broccoli?
If I'm virtuous as a marigold, dour as denial,
will I live to 99? This is my decline,
I pluck processed bonbons, a few a day,
from pleated paper veils, taste is life!
How delicious they look displayed
in their ribboned sarcophagus.

The Body Takes the Soul for a Walk

My fingers press button into buttonhole
slide thump next
feet avoid dog piss
as a I breathe each step.
Sunlight lifts something
more than stride
first green, forsythia—
winter died.
I need another spring.
I need another spring.

Venus on the Hudson

There is a green music
before orange sun sparks off the Hudson's
fluttered surface and dulls behind New Jersey.

Riverside Park makes me want to run naked—

I invoke my 17-year-old self
running tenderly on the pliant grass and thrusting roots
hiding finding in the shadows my lover, my self
flinging ourselves in the light we forget everything
but our incandescence
in the field behind the school
years later I found out we had an audience.

I can't be embarrassed.
It wasn't me, but the spirit of summer.

A Sonnet on Not Selling Many Books

Each step, the new snow groans beneath my heel
unh unh unh, while my dog's cookie cutter
paws soundlessly pattern the sidewalk reel
of dog daily news, in piss and litter.
I fear the covering over, iced air,
God, let word outlast receding footprints.
Books one and two sold just to those who care
I spoke to myself, no experiments...
in my woman's voice and white woman's life
much humor, childbirth, and domestic tears...
meaning unman, sans scotch, tenure, and wife.
I wanted no academic career.
Which brings me back to the locked door.
Where's the key? I don't have it anymore.

Fuck Cancer 1

I want go back to 1976, just for a week, when I was making out
with too many boys and figuring out how to write a real essay.

I felt so debased, wicked—getting stoned, drunk, waking up
next to someone I couldn't name or despise. Despair chasing joy
all through the gray quads, sharp lectures, and learning
the fraught or sweet ways my body could please and take.

I was cut loose from my mother; buried in Brooklyn that spring,
from my past in too many places to count on two hands.
I changed majors, partners, breaking-up so I could open my grief
with Yeats and Plath in the thin pages of my Norton anthology.

I worried about exhibiting mediocrity—as I carried a real human
   skull
in my backpack so I could draw my own *memento mori* over the
   weekend
and consider if poetry or anthropology were the better way to
   calibrate death.
I want to cry over the messy becoming, not this tidy medicated
   undoing.

Fuck Cancer 2

Friends, I can hear you cringe as you ask
"How are you?" A year ago, I would have
shivered too, as stepping into a draft
from a window that never fully closes.

I see my face hanging on or outside the glass
the wisps of my new white hair
make me a moon above Broadway
with Grandmother's cratered eyes.

The body goes on as well as it can
until it can't. Somehow, I never believed
despite the pets eased into the last injection,
the falls and springs speeding into streaked newsreels.

I drift away from my distractions: novels, chocolates,
wine, flirtations... as I wane, as I bend into a sickle.

Poems for Deborah

1

Your departure fits this season of twigs
clutching their furled leaves against the stern wind
that sweeps away half-finished novels, sheaves
of legal paper, our conversations.
I speak to you on the trails of my dreams...
my soul's too rational to hear your voice.
Wind knocks each tree from sultry to sentry.
I haven't kept a diary in years,
our adventures as middle aged writers
purveyors of easier to reach arts
can't endure in the shedding library
of my memory...yet I keep wanting
to call you or visit, to say...Debbie,
if not facts, the gist, warms me these cold days.

2

If not the facts, the gist warms me these cold days
I'm to live awhile, months or perhaps years
in a half poisoned stasis: health half full!
Oh, we laughed at being told we were brave,
as if loving and breathing were a choice.
Sick and sainted, in haloes of wishes.
Please don't make me a mascot of demise.
Cancer can't steal irreverence and snark!
But death takes everything and nothing less
than a band of mourners and works remain.
I was thought to go first, you chased a cure,
my odds were worse, chance is a pretty curse.
And now you know I've lied, you showed me how
to die with care and grace despite your fears.

3

Dear Debbie, how can you be dying
on a night of civil unrest, helicopters and sirens?

You who spoke softly or not at all
a social smile for a reserved heart
observations saved for later, sharpened by wit.

I thought you deserved some sweeter notes
than shouts and municipal budgets gone to riot squads...

Let us hear the arias and songs you were writing.

How can you leave now with your novel half finished—
what will Captain Leonie do without you
to guide *The Water Lizard* to new plot points?

With my heart half emptied
the streets are empty now too
the protesters gone to bed...
Life is so short and yet I found you
let that be the better sorrow
I found you and loved you
and you had to leave too soon.
No wonder the sky rings with grief.

4

Saying goodbye while you can still listen

But cannot speak or move, eyes shut

As any marble effigy, oh friend

I spoke to you half in eulogy

Half as if you were listening for the door buzzer

to deliver dinner...

But no, we're not on the phone, each at home

With our families about to swirl

Our attention to TV or who wants to drink what.

No, your choices are gone.

How frightened you must be

With tests and procedures hurting and your eyes and

Voice gone. I spoke of our friendship

Half to you, half to your daughter in law

Did you hear? Was I insufferable?

I try to be sincere, dying demands it.

What truth remains? You suffer

Into release, nothing I say can ease

This hard dark wrenching. Love

Is sweet but fear and pain strong.

Your tipped head and swollen fingers.

No justice in it.

The novel you were writing, the lyrics,

Stories...it ends. We each bring all our possibles

To the last hour. If I could be you and finish

The tale, but you always surprised me.
No you didn't like Meryl Streep, yes you watched
Shows like Grimm that I couldn't watch...

5

It's been over a month Debbie, I can
imagine your vacation in the U.K.
visiting your half brother, or you run
a fundraising workshop in St. Tropez.

Say we haven't talked since I am away
in smoggy Beijing with another of
my husbands translated musicals. Play
with reasons why, heart feels the stretch of love

calls not made, emails not received, your couch
where I sat and sipped the coffee as we
talked perils of treatments and wills crouched.

And on, and on

Two months, a day, a breath
and the time of you
becomes time ago

Time is a scrim
shuddering in invisible hands
as the scene repaints itself

The scene feels like habit until
a show ends, a restaurant closes,
the crouched winter sun rises.

The sun will rise to spring
you won't be here to feel the breeze
lift the new green scent.

You are, you were, sent away
but my habit of remembering you
will last for months, days, my lifetime.

Ride

Go stand at the door, see death drive
His Lamborghini, with room for one.
Is it you tonight? How dark are the windows
And white the steering wheel, he honks for you
To come, come down and take your ride
The seats are velvet, and dead or alive
He drives in the HOV lane when you're inside.

Driving Lessons

There's a wheeze my lungs make
a half whistle, as if a smaller version
of me nestled inside, drawing attention
to her mortality and tin ear. I don't want
that tune buried in my ear, Venus still
twangs the cat gut upside, useless
unless we decide to wind up the model F
for a ride of grumps and grinding
fears, it's been a year of modeling
the latest shrouds, filmy eyes.
Can I not think of imminent demise
for five minutes? Or even the seven
seconds when sparks combust
radiomind, I'd like that, I'd like that.
Before I collide with the wall that isn't there.

Dirty Laundry

Eros is limply pegged to the clothesline,
boil and wring, sun and bleach, he's not the thing
that kept you and another spinning time
lips and hips, slip and flow, until the ring
of morning sent you both sundered in joy.
Sidewalks, gutters, bushes sang sex to you
flies and woodpeckers, didn't diddle coy.
Feet lift, throb swings? Only felt in the blues
oh yeah, oh yeah, go wear those yearning notes...
If you could have saved a stash of those hours
or would switch partners the way you switch coats
but threadbare lust is the cost as life scours
the juicy color from your skin and heart.
Too old, too sick, too true, for a new start.

Random Abdominal Tumors

The staircase is supported by rust-thinned struts
so thin I could tap it apart with a nudge
The concrete stairs wobble in their cracked subsections
I think: will this be the day 20 commuters and I die
Trying to achieve 28th street and 7th avenue?
Will we be crushed going up towards the light
Or buried in the latrine of the tiled echo?

Something wails down the tubes.
Something pushes the air out.
It will be here and gone before
I can think of another analogy.

2nd Brain MRI

Between the noose
and the hood
a world to love

Between the bud
and falling petals
my daughters

The cornea of the sky
holds back the stars in their multitude
keeps us human.

Pickup

My mother's foreign cars were prone to metal fatigue
exhaust pipes dropped off, gas caps shrugged loose.
Rust clawed the doors like a dog trapped in a closet.
Worst were the cogs and thump rockets inside
when some shaft or screw would peel apart and the
little car would bang or choke and go slow
and slower still and we'd coast to the curb
of human kindness. We'd wait, hood up,
lights flashing, Mom's elbow out the window
and after our obligatory stream of *goddamits*
we'd discuss the movie we watched last night,
or I'd say, once the car is fixed can we go to
the craft store since I'm out of orange yarn
for crocheting squares for my granny blanket,
or she'd tell me about playing stickball in Flatbush
when cars were higher off the road
and a skinny tomboy could find her
home run ball easier under a Studebaker...
Then a tap on her door, always a man,
"Ma'm, can I help you with this car,
give you (noticing me) and the little girl a lift?"
And I saw how they saw her, the dazzle
of black curls and quirked rosebud lips

dark eyes darkly lashed, laughing,
body trim, but bust a full C cup...
She became another style of woman, kinda flirty,
perplexed about How Things Worked, engine-wise,
thank goodness you came along just then...
She'd amuse as the man drove me to school
amuse as he dropped her off at the garage
that knew well the failings of our car,
I'm sure he tried to give her his number
or extract a hint that the divorcee was willing.
She'd smile her crooked smile
and say, thank you but I'm too busy
with a little girl to raise,
meaning, I prefer women,
or at least the kind of men
that don't help strangers
in exchange for favors.

Agony Aunt's Toolkit for Young Women

Sometimes my sunny Caitlin
has a scream caught in her eyes.

I want to give her a woman's toolkit
for tinkering with common assholery:

She'd have an adjustable wrench (twist it tight)
for every guy trying to make her a fuck-a-night wench;

A ball peen hammer and memory nails
for flaky friends, *oh—I forgot*, who stand her up;

A gray matter rasp for removing budding habits
from roommates, dates, parents, and cats;

For fine tuning of lovers I'd bequeath pneumatic levers,
to modulate levels of gassy opinion and lovesick gazes;

Co-workers and bosses need the gentle correction
a tip, a tap, of chainsaws and mallets;

But most of all, I'd weld a bullhorn to fit her mouth
and force her to shout, shout, and spit it out.

Living It

Read a true story about a woman
who hadn't smiled in forty years
to keep her face young,
and it was, except for her eyes
where all the smiles and frowns
must have gone
to die

and I
think of my daughter Natalie
who has laughed more in this last year
of finding love and new career, laughed more
than the past three of her 20s

and already faint quote marks
frame her mobile lips
and as she complains five white hairs
invaded her scalp I know
her perfectly freckled gorgeous face
will
escape
unmarked perfection.

Side Effects

I'm dizzy, I'm pale
as ginger ale
swelling like a lemon
in the garden
of my couch.

I crouch
like a cabbage
frost ragged
but won't quit.

You and I quip
laugh and gripe
staked to this frail life.
Send us some spring
send me into spring.

Sweet Dreams

The air and sky wake me to the world
      Even as I struggle to push the wheel chair
         Two blocks and then sit and allow
     Natalie and Chris to push me home.
People walk fast or slowly, their dogs too.
     Shop keepers come out to tell me
        God or Jesus or other deities will help
    And I simply thank them since I have no faith in
Santa saviors. I believe in fall afternoons.
     The yellows of the leaves are lemons
        Against the blue and gray tablecloth of sky.
How lucky I am despite weakening.

Visiting Gallery

My parents, breathing and not,
sit with me in the living room.
I am queen of the couch
languid on pillows
as unpain pills muffle
gut cramps and tumor twists.

This second toddlerhood
means I crave soft bland things
Jello for god's sake
and mom #2 cheers when I poo.

My ghost mom shakes her head
only 43, tapping her foot,
sorrow and I told you so
as she puffs clouds of clouds.

I love them, in their old age
and afterlife, how real it is
having to say goodbye
in the wrong order to my living
loving father and mother.
I wish I didn't have to hurt them.
Couldn't the cancer have waited?

About the Author

CLAUDIA CARLSON was born in Bloomington, Indiana, grew up in academic neighborhoods across the US, and lived in Manhattan since she was 22. She majored in English and Art History at SUNY Stony Brook. Her first poetry book, *The Elephant House*, was published by Marsh Hawk Press in 2007 and in 2013 a photo/poetry book, *Pocket Park*, came out. With Jeanne Marie Beaumont, she helped edit the fairy tale anthology *The Poets' Grimm*, Story Line Press 2003. Carlson conceived, wrote, and illustrated the picture book *Avi the Ambulance Goes to School* to help promote the life-saving work of Magen David Adom, part of the International Red Cross, Apples&Honey Press/Behrman House, 2015. *Avi the Ambulance to the Rescue* is forthcoming in 2016. Most of her working career was spent as a graphic artist designing book covers and interiors in publishing houses (web design at MTV and Meryl Lynch), and she designed the award-winning magazine *Alimentum the Literature of Food*. Carlson also had several one-woman shows for her portraits and photos. She's married to playwright and lyricist James Racheff. Both of her daughters, Natalie and Caitlin, are involved in the arts.

TITLES FROM MARSH HAWK PRESS

Jane Augustine, KRAZY: Visual Poems and Performance Scripts, A Woman's Guide to Mountain Climbing, Night Lights, Arbor Vitae

Thomas Beckett, ~~DIPSTICK~~ (DIPTYCH)

Sigman Byrd, Under the Wanderer's Star

Patricia Carlin, Quantum Jitters, Original Green

Claudia Carlson, My Chocolate Sarcophagus, Pocket Park, The Elephant House

Meredith Cole, Miniatures

Jon Curley, Hybrid Moments

Neil de la Flor, An Elephant's Memory of Blizzards, Almost Dorothy

Chard deNiord, Sharp Golden Thorn

Sharon Dolin, Serious Pink

Steve Fellner, The Weary World Rejoices, Blind Date with Cavafy

Thomas Fink, Joyride, Peace Conference, Clarity and Other Poems, After Taxes, Gossip: A Book of Poems

Norman Finkelstein, Inside the Ghost Factory, Passing Over

Edward Foster, Dire Straits,The Beginning of Sorrows,What He Ought To Know, Mahrem: Things Men Should Do for Men

Paolo Javier, The Feeling Is Actual

Burt Kimmelman, Somehow

Burt Kimmelman and Fred Caruso, The Pond at Cape May Point

Basil King, The Spoken Word/the Painted Hand from Learning to Draw/A History 77 Beasts: Basil King's Bestiary, Mirage

Martha King, Imperfect Fit

Phillip Lopate, At the End of the Day: Selected Poems and An Introductory Essay

Mary Mackey, Travelers With No Ticket Home, Sugar Zone, Breaking the Fever

Jason McCall, Dear Hero,

Sandy McIntosh, Cemetery Chess: Selected and New Poems, Ernesta, in the Style of the Flamenco, Forty-Nine Guaranteed Ways to Escape Death, The After-Death History of My Mother, Between Earth and Sky

Stephen Paul Miller, There's Only One God and You're Not It, Fort Dad, The Bee Flies in May, Skinny Eighth Avenue, Any Lie You Tell Will Be the Truth

Daniel Morris, If Not for the Courage, Bryce Passage, Hit Play

Sharon Olinka, The Good City

Christina Olivares, No Map of the Earth Includes Stars

Justin Petropoulos, Eminent Domain

Paul Pines, Charlotte Songs, Divine Madness, Last Call at the Tin Palace

Jacquelyn Pope, Watermark

George Quasha, Things Done For Themselves

Karin Randolph, Either She Was

Rochelle Ratner, Ben Casey Days, Balancing Acts, House and Home

Michael Rerick, In Ways Impossible to Fold

Corrine Robins, Facing It: New and Selected Poems, Today's Menu, One Thousand Years

Eileen R. Tabios, Sun Stigmata, The Thorn Rosary: Selected Prose Poems and New (1998–2010), The Light Sang As It Left Your Eyes: Our Autobiography, I Take Thee, English, for My Beloved, Reproductions of the Empty Flagpole

Eileen R. Tabios and j/j hastain, the relational elations of ORPHANED ALGEBRA

Susan Terris, Ghost of Yesterday, Natural Defenses

Madeline Tiger, Birds of Sorrow and Joy

Tana Jean Welch, Latest Volcano

Harriet Zinnes, New and Selected Poems, Weather Is Whether, Light Light or the Curvature of the Earth, Whither Nonstopping, Drawing on the Wall

YEAR	AUTHOR	MHP POETRY PRIZE TITLE	JUDGE
2004	Jacquelyn Pope	Watermark	Marie Ponsot
2005	Sigman Byrd	Under the Wanderer's Star	Gerald Stern
2006	Steve Fellner	Blind Date With Cavafy	Denise Duhamel
2007	Karin Randolph	Either She Was	David Shapiro
2008	Michael Rerick	In Ways Impossible to Fold	Thylias Moss
2009	Neil de la Flor	Almost Dorothy	Forrest Gander
2010	Justin Petropoulos	Eminent Domain	Anne Waldman
2011	Meredith Cole	Miniatures	Alicia Ostriker
2012	Jason McCall	Dear Hero,	Cornelius Eady
2013	Tom Beckett	~~DIPSTICK~~ (DIPTYCH)	Charles Bernstein
2014	Christina Olivares	No Map of the Earth Includes Stars	Brenda Hillman
2015	Tana Jean Welch	Latest Volcano	Stephanie Strickland

ARTISTIC ADVISORY BOARD

Toi Derricotte, Denise Duhamel, Marilyn Hacker, Allan Kornblum (in memorium), Maria Mazzioti Gillan, Alicia Ostriker, Marie Ponsot, David Shapiro, Nathaniel Tarn, Anne Waldman, and John Yau.

For more information, please go to: **www.marshhawkpress.org**